THE MOST REQUESTED
Jazz Standards

JAZZ

Cherry Lane Music Company
Director of Publications/Project Editor: Mark Phillips

ISBN 978-1-60378-976-9

Visit our website at www.cherrylaneprint.com

CONTENTS

Ain't Misbehavin'

Words by Andy Razaf

Music by
Thomas "Fats" Waller and Harry Brooks

Boy: Though it's a fick - le
Girl: Your type of man is

age, With flirt - ing all the rage,
rare, I know you real - ly care,

for, be - lieve me. I don't stay out late,

don't care to go, I'm home a - bout eight, just me and my ra - di - o.

Ain't mis - be - hav - in', I'm sav - in' my love for you.

you. _____

All the Things You Are

from VERY WARM FOR MAY

Lyrics by Oscar Hammerstein II

Music by Jerome Kern

Moderately

Time and a-gain I've longed for ad-ven-ture, some-thing to make my

heart beat the fast-er. What did I long for? I nev-er real-ly

knew. Find-ing your love, I've found my ad-ven-ture;

Basin Street Blues

Words and Music by
Spencer Williams

Blame It on My Youth

Words by Edward Heyman

Music by Oscar Levant

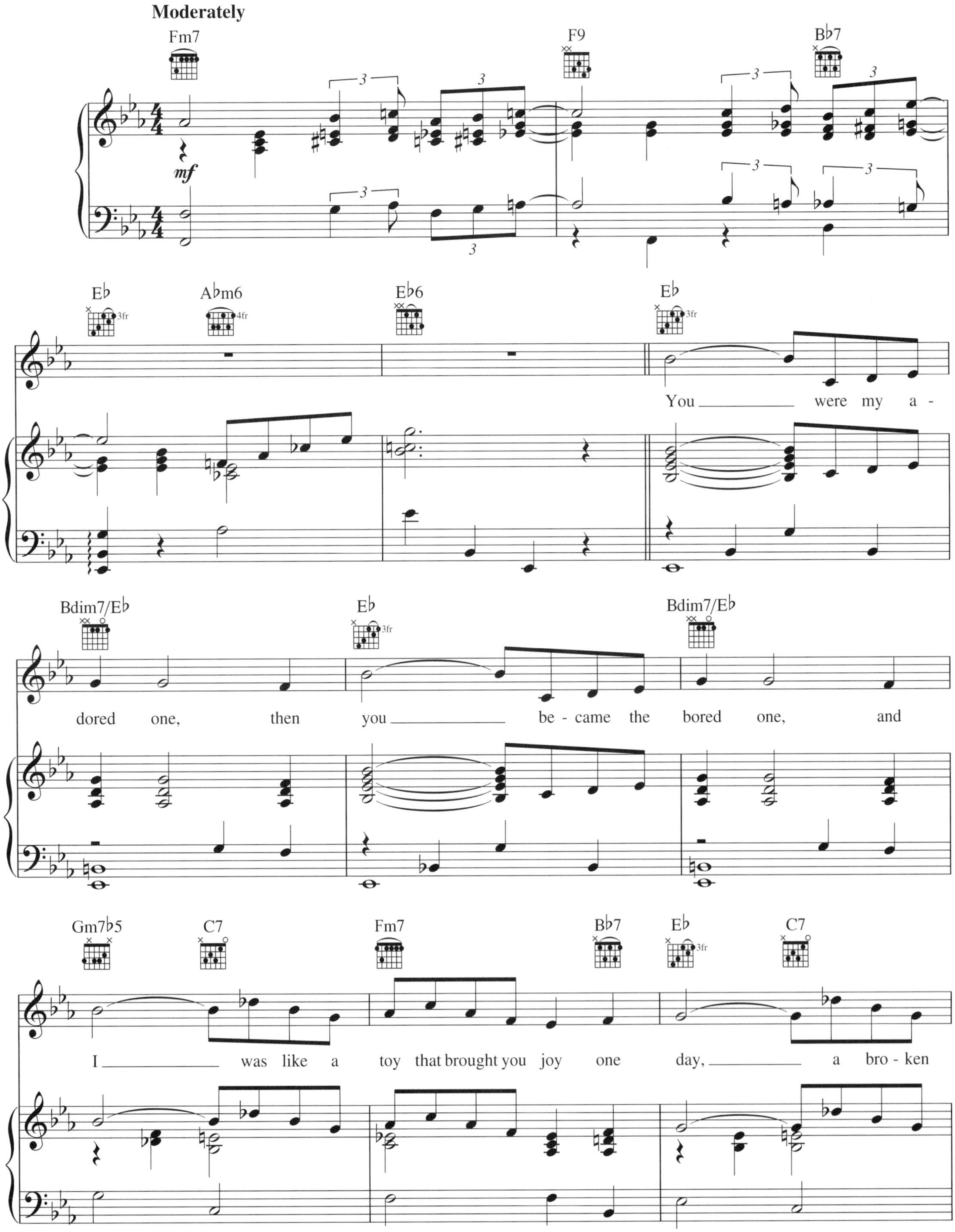

Lyrics:

You _____ were my a- dored one, then you _____ be-came the bored one, and I _____ was like a toy that brought you joy one day, _____ a bro-ken

pray, blame it on my youth. ___ If _____ I cried a

lit - tle bit when first I learned the truth,

don't blame it on my heart, ___ blame it on my youth. ___

Blue Skies

from BETSY

Words and Music by
Irving Berlin

Bluesette

Words by Norman Gimbel

Music by Jean Thielemans

Moderate Waltz

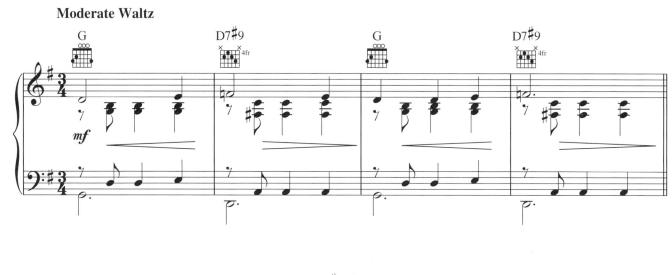

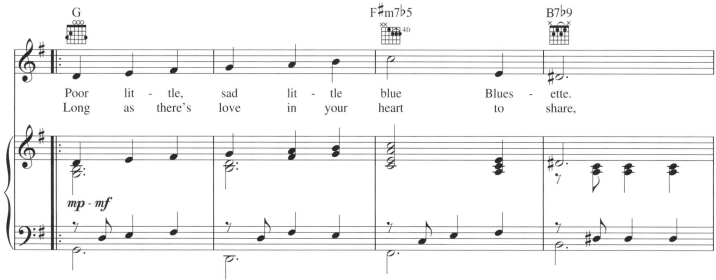

Poor lit - tle, sad lit - tle blue Blues - ette.
Long as there's love in your heart Blues to share,

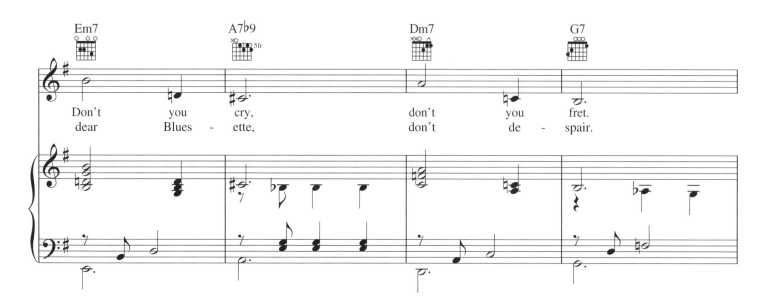

Don't you cry, don't you fret.
dear Blues - ette, don't de - spair.

Cmaj7   C6   Cm7   F7

Love wrapped in rain - bows and tied with pink rib - bon to

B♭maj7   B♭6   B♭m7   E♭7

make your next Spring - time your gold wed - ding ring time. So,

A♭   Am7♭5   D7

dry your eyes. Don't - cha pout, don't - cha fret, good - y

Bm7   B♭7   Am7   D7

good times are com - ing, Blues - ette.

One luck - y day, love - ly love will come your way. That mag - ic day may just be to - day.

molto rit.

But Beautiful

from ROAD TO RIO

Words by Johnny Burke

Music by Jimmy Van Heusen

But Not for Me

from GIRL CRAZY

Music and Lyrics by
George Gershwin and Ira Gershwin

Rather slow *(smoothly)*

Bye Bye Blackbird
from PETE KELLY'S BLUES

Lyric by Mort Dixon

Music by Ray Henderson

Can't Help Lovin' Dat Man

from SHOW BOAT

Lyrics by Oscar Hammerstein II

Music by Jerome Kern

de an - gels done plan.

De chimb-ley's smok - in', de roof is leak - in' in, _____ but he don't _____ seem to care. _____ He can be hap-py 'wid jus' a sip of gin. _____ I e - ven loves him when _____

back dat day is fine, _____ de sun will shine.

He can come home _ as late as can be; ___ home wid-out him _ ain't

no home to me. ___ Can't help lov-in' dat man _ of

mine.

mine. _____

Cheek to Cheek

from the RKO Radio Motion Picture TOP HAT

Words and Music by
Irving Berlin

seem to find the hap - pi - ness I seek _____ when we're

out to - geth - er danc - ing cheek _ to cheek. _

Heav - en, _____ I'm in Heav - en. _____ And the cares that hung a -

round me through the week _____ seem to van - ish like a gam - bler's luck - y

streak _____ when we're out to-geth - er danc - ing cheek _ to cheek. _

_____ Oh, I love to climb a moun - tain, and to

reach the high-est peak, ___ but it does - n't thrill me half as much _ as

danc - ing cheek to cheek. ___ Oh, I love to go out fish - ing in a

Come Fly with Me

Words by Sammy Cahn

Music by James Van Heusen

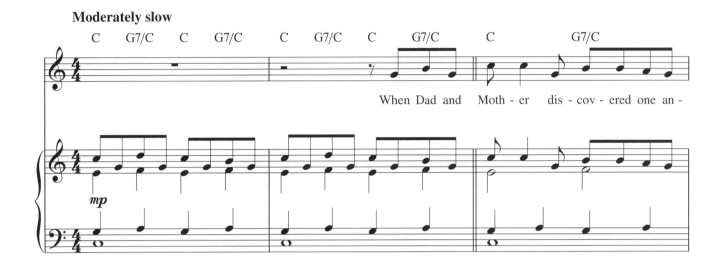

When Dad and Moth - er dis-cov - ered one an -

oth - er, they dreamed of the day when they would love and hon - or and o -

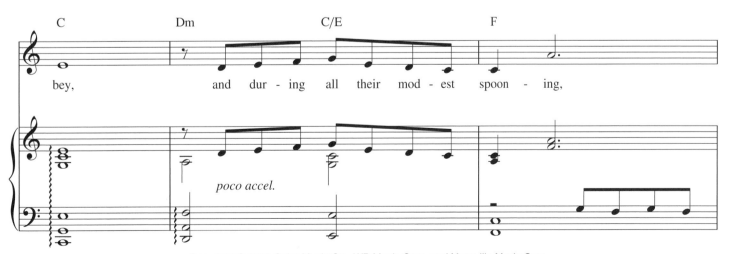

bey, and dur - ing all their mod - est spoon - ing,

they'd blush and speak of hon - ey - moon - ing. And if your mem - o - ry re -

calls, they spoke of Ni - ag - 'ra Falls. _____ But to -

day, my dar - ling, to - day, when you meet the one you love, you

Moderately, with a strong beat

say: _____ Come fly with me! ___ Let's fly!

In Lla - ma Land _ there's a one - man band _ and he'll toot his flute for you. Come fly with me! _ Let's take _ off in _ the blue! _ Once I get you up there, _ where the air is rar - i - fied, _ we'll just glide, _

say the words __ and we'll beat the birds __ down to Ac - a - pul - co Bay. It's per - fect for __ a fly - ing hon - ey - moon, they say. Come fly with me! __ Let's fly! __ Let's fly __ a - way! _____ Come way! _____

Come Rain or Come Shine

from ST. LOUIS WOMAN

Words by Johnny Mercer

Music by Harold Arlen

Darn That Dream

Lyric by Eddie De Lange

Music by Jimmy Van Heusen

Darn that dream I
Darn your dream lips and

dream each night, you say you love me and you
darn your eyes, they say lift me high a - bove the

hold me tight, but when I a - wake you're
moon - lit skies, then I tum - ble out of

Dearly Beloved

from YOU WERE NEVER LOVELIER

Words by Johnny Mercer

Music by Jerome Kern

Easy Living
Theme from the Paramount Picture EASY LIVING

Words and Music by
Leo Robin and Ralph Rainger

Embraceable You

from CRAZY FOR YOU

Music and Lyrics by
George Gershwin and Ira Gershwin

Em - brace me, you ir - re - place - a - ble you! _____

Just one look at you, my heart grew tip - sy in me; _____

you and you a - lone bring out the gyp - sy in me! _____

I love all the man - y charms a - bout you; _____

Emily

from the MGM Motion Picture THE AMERICANIZATION OF EMILY

Words by Johnny Mercer

Music by Johnny Mandel

Fascinating Rhythm

from RHAPSODY IN BLUE

Music and Lyrics by
George Gershwin and Ira Gershwin

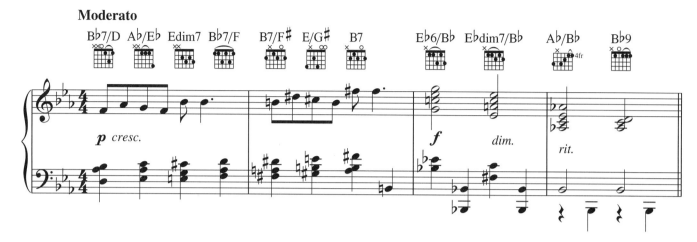

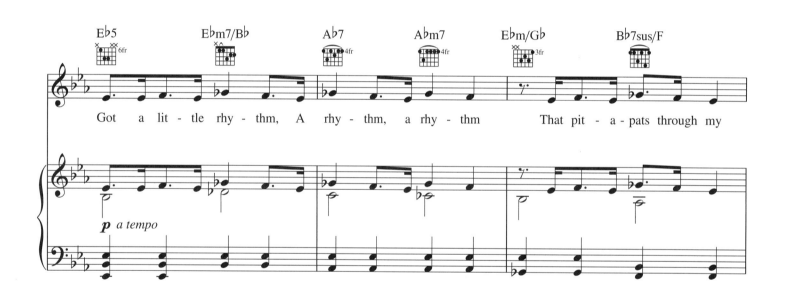

Got a lit-tle rhy-thm, A rhy-thm, a rhy-thm That pit-a-pats through my

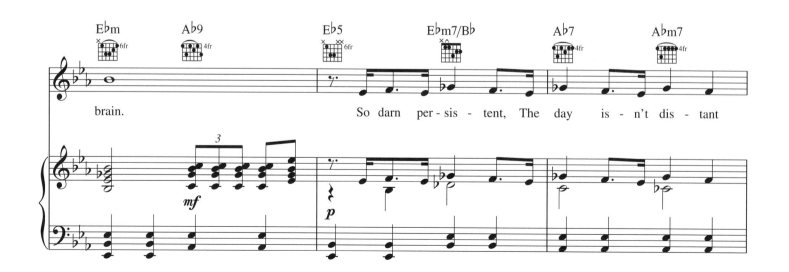

brain.   So darn per-sis-tent, The day is-n't dis-tant

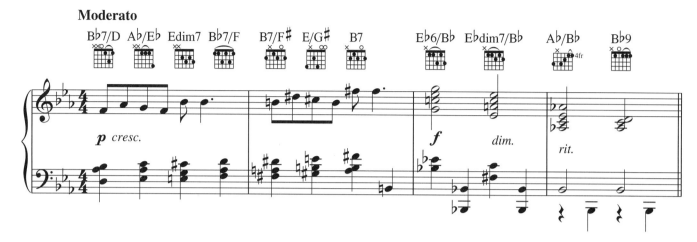

Fly Me to the Moon
(In Other Words)

Words and Music by
Bart Howard

Bossa Nova

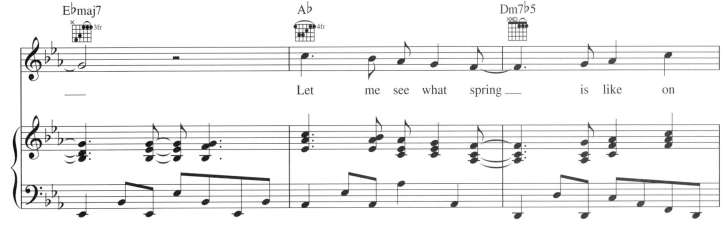

Fly me to the moon, ___ and let me play a - mong the stars; ___

___ Let me see what spring ___ is like on

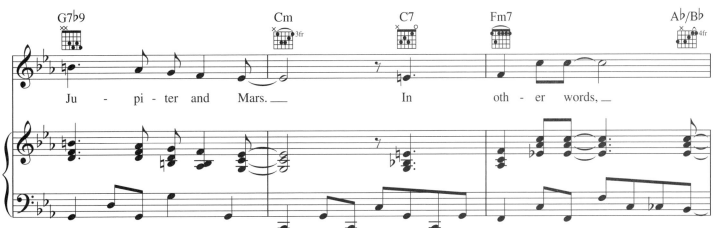

Ju - pi - ter and Mars. ___ In oth - er words, ___

A Foggy Day

(In London Town)

from A DAMSEL IN DISTRESS

Music and Lyrics by
George Gershwin and Ira Gershwin

Georgia on My Mind

Words by Stuart Gorrell

Music by Hoagy Carmichael

The Glory of Love

Words and Music by
Billy Hill

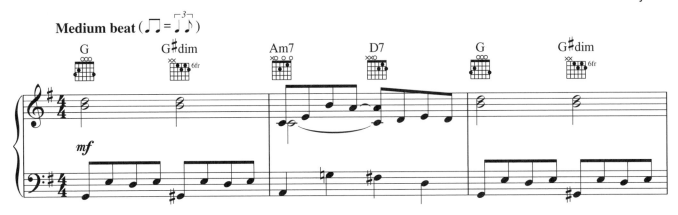

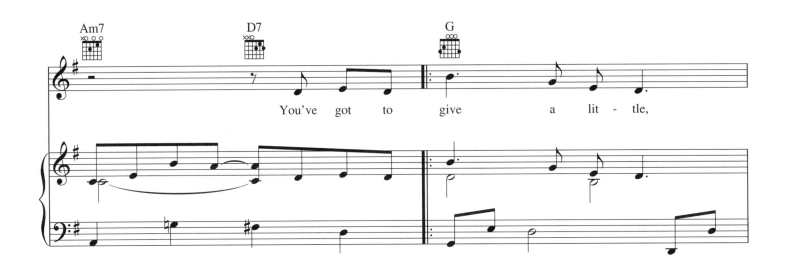

You've got to give a lit - tle,

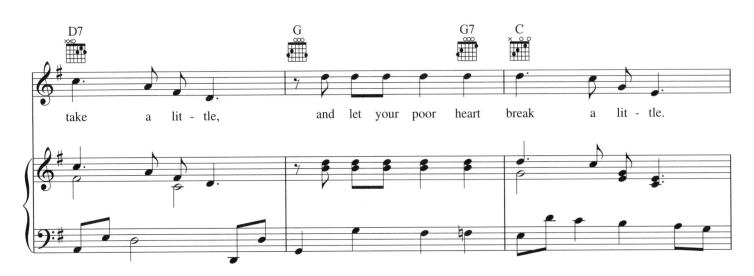

take a lit - tle, and let your poor heart break a lit - tle.

God Bless the Child

Words and Music by
Arthur Herzog Jr. and Billie Holiday

Slowly, with feeling

Here's That Rainy Day

from CARNIVAL IN FLANDERS

Words by Johnny Burke

Music by Jimmy Van Heusen

How About You?

Words by Ralph Freed

Music by Burton Lane

B7#5

will de - pend on lit - tle plea - sures they will share.

G   G6   Gdim7   Am7   D7   Am7   D6 D7

So   let   us   com - pare.

Moderately, with expression

G6   Gmaj7   G/B   Bbdim7   Am7

I   like   New   York   in   June,   how   a - bout   you? __

D7   G6   Gmaj7   G/B   F#7

__   I   like   a   Gersh - win   tune,

And Frank - lin Roose - velt's looks, give me a thrill. ___

___ Hold - ing hands in a mov - ie show, when all the lights are low

may not be new. But I like it, how a - bout

you? you? _____

How Deep Is the Ocean
(How High Is the Sky)

Words and Music by
Irving Berlin

I Can't Give You Anything but Love

from BLACKBIRDS OF 1928

Words and Music by
Jimmy McHugh and Dorothy Fields

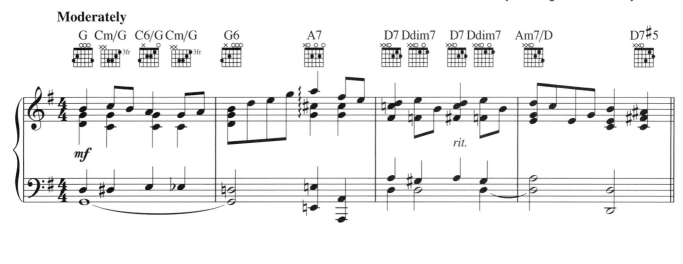

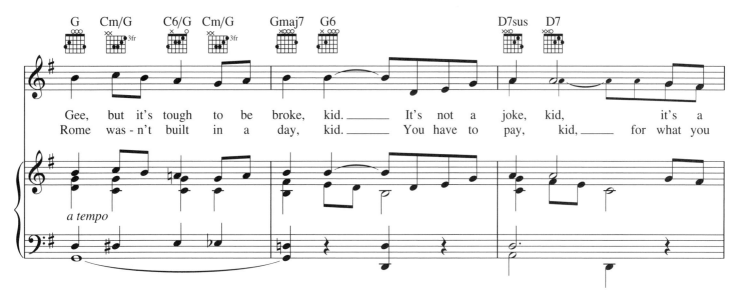

Gee, but it's tough to be broke, kid. ____ It's not a joke, kid, it's a
Rome was-n't built in a day, kid. ____ You have to pay, kid, ____ for what you

curse.
get.

My luck is chang-ing, it's got-ten ____ from sim-ply
But I am will-ing to wait, dear; ____ your lit-tle

rot - ten _____ to some-thing worse. Who knows, some-day I will
mate, dear, _____ will not for - get. You have a life - time be -

win, too. I'll be - gin to reach my prime.
fore you. I'll a - dore you, come what may.

Now, though I see what our end is, _____ all I can spend is just my
Please don't be blue for the pres - ent, _____ when it's so pleas - ant _____ to hear you

time.
say: } I can't give you an - y - thing but love,

ba - by.   That's the on - ly thing I've plen - ty of,

ba - by.   Dream a-while,   scheme a-while;   we're sure to find __

__   hap - pi - ness   and I guess   all those things you've

al - ways pined for.   Gee, I'd like to see you look - ing

swell, ba - by; dia - mond brace - lets Wool - worth does - n't

sell, ba - by. Till that luck - y day, you know darned

well, ba - by, I can't give you an - y - thing but

love. love. _____

114

I Get a Kick Out of You

from ANYTHING GOES

Words and Music by
Cole Porter

The on - ly ex - cep - tion I know is the case _____ _____ when I'm out on a qui - et spree ___ fight - ing vain - ly the old en - nui, ___ and I sud - den - ly turn and see ___ your fab - u - lous face.

I Got Rhythm

from AN AMERICAN IN PARIS

Music and Lyrics by
George Gershwin and Ira Gershwin

'Round ___ my door. I ___ got star- light, ___ I ___ got sweet dreams, ___ I ___ got my man ___ Who could ask for an-y-thing more, Who could ask for an-y-thing more? more?

I Won't Dance

from ROBERTA

Words and Music by
Jimmy McHugh, Dorothy Fields,
Jerome Kern, Oscar Hammerstein II
and Otto Harbach

Think of what you're los-ing by con-stant-ly re-fus-ing to dance with me. _____

_____ You'd be the i-dol of France with me! _____ And yet you stand there and

shake your fool-ish head dra-mat-i-c'lly. While I wait here

so ec - stat - i - c'lly you just look and say em - phat - i - c'lly

not this sea - son! There's a rea - son!

I won't dance! Don't ask me. I won't dance!

Don't ask me. I won't dance, ma - dame, with

bumped on the shore. _____ I feel so ab-so-lute-ly

stumped on the floor! _____

She: When you dance you're charm-ing and you're gen - tle! _____

_____ 'Spec - 'lly when you do the "Con - ti -

nen - tal." _____ *He:* But this feel - ing

is - n't pure - ly men - tal. _____ For heav - en

rest us, _____ I'm not as - bes - tos. _____

___ And that's why I won't dance! Why should I?

I'll Be Around

Words and Music by
Alec Wilder

I'll Remember April

Words and Music by
Pat Johnston, Don Raye
and Gene De Paul

Moderately, with expression

I'm Beginning to See the Light

Words and Music by
Don George, Johnny Hodges,
Duke Ellington and Harry James

140

If I Were a Bell

from GUYS AND DOLLS

By Frank Loesser

mo - ment we kissed to - night ___ that's the way I've just got to be - have. ___ Boy, if
knew my mo - rale would crack ___ from the won - der - ful way that you looked. ___ Boy, if

I were a lamp I'd light, ___ or if I ___ were a ban - ner I'd wave. ___
I were a duck I'd quack, ___ or if I ___ were a goose ___ I'd be cooked. ___

Ask me how do I feel, ___ lit - tle me with my qui - et up -
Ask me how do I feel, ___ ask me now that we're fond - ly ca -

bring - ing. _____ Well, sir, all I can say ___ is if I ___
ress - ing. _____ Pal, if I were a sal - ad I know ___

143

In the Wee Small Hours of the Morning

Words by Bob Hilliard

Music by David Mann

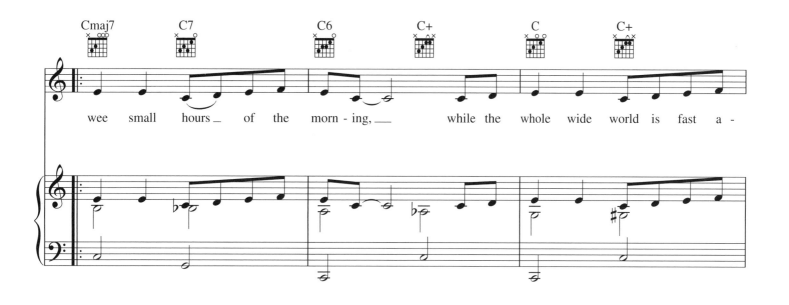

wee small hours _ of the morn - ing, ___ while the whole wide world is fast a -

sleep, you lie a - wake and think a - bout the { girl, } and
{ boy, }

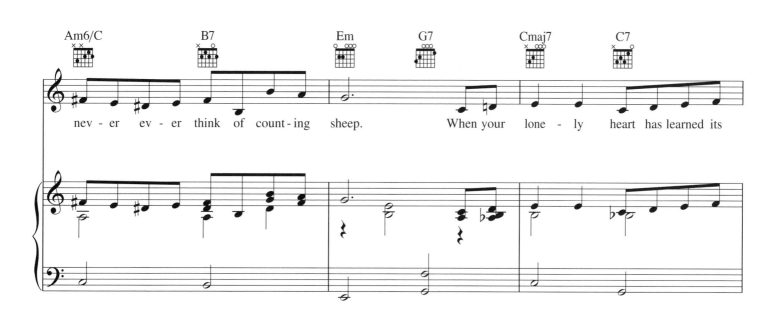

nev - er ev - er think of count - ing sheep. When your lone - ly heart has learned its

It Don't Mean a Thing

(If It Ain't Got That Swing)

from SOPHISTICATED LADIES

Words and Music by
Duke Ellington and Irving Mills

Vamp

What good is mel-o-dy, ___ what good is mu-sic, ___ if it ain't pos-sess-in' some-thing

It Had to Be You

Words by Gus Kahn

Music by Isham Jones

why don't I try ___ to for - get? It must have
It's up to you ___ to ex - plain. I'm think - ing

been that some - thing lov - ers call fate ___ kept on say - ing
may - be, ba - by, I'll go a - way, ___ some - day, some way,

I had to wait. ___ I saw them all, ___ just could-n't fall ___ 'til we
you'll come and say: ___ "It's you I need, ___ and you'll be plead - ing in

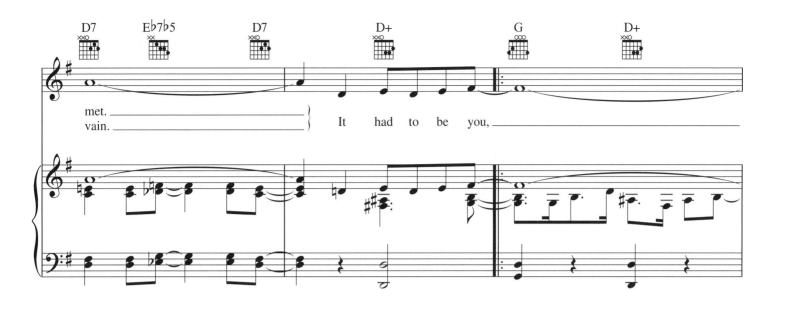

met. _____
vain. _____ } It had to be you, _____

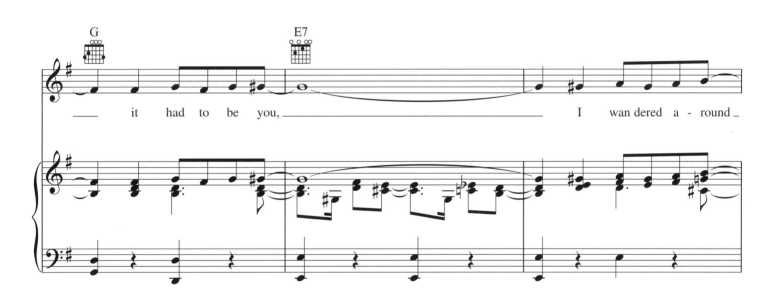

_____ it had to be you, _____ I wan dered a - round _

_____ and fi - nal - ly found _____ the some-bod - y who _____

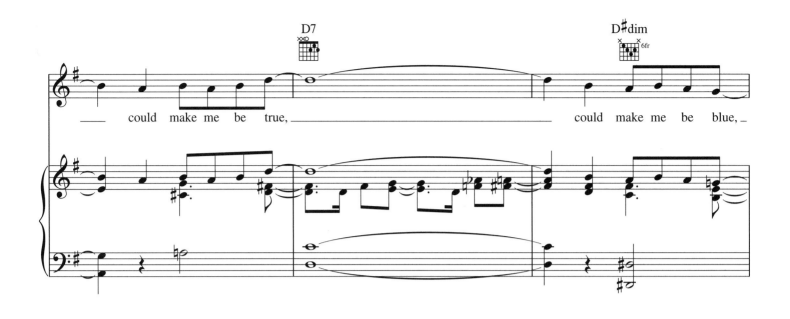

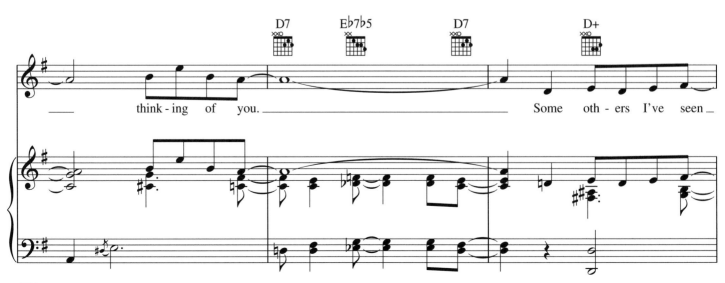

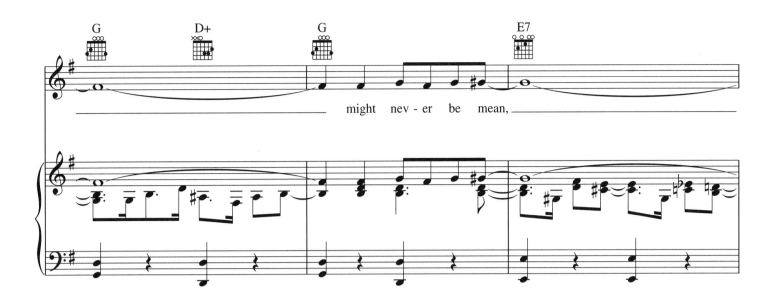

might nev - er be mean,

might nev - er be cross ___ or try to be boss, ___ but they would-n't do. ___

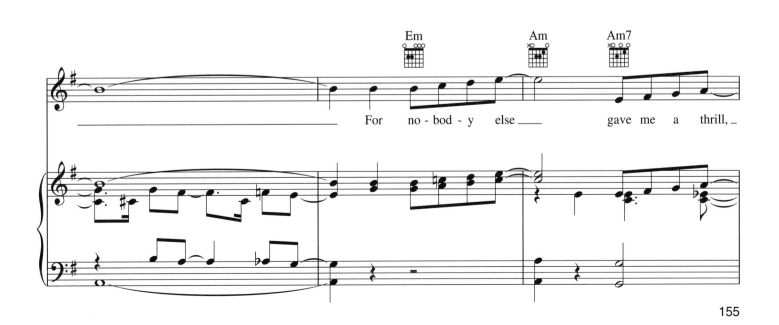

For no - bod - y else ___ gave me a thrill, _

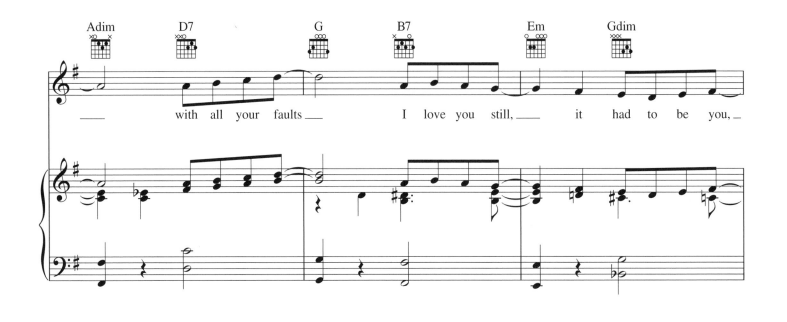

with all your faults ___ I love you still, ___ it had to be you, ___

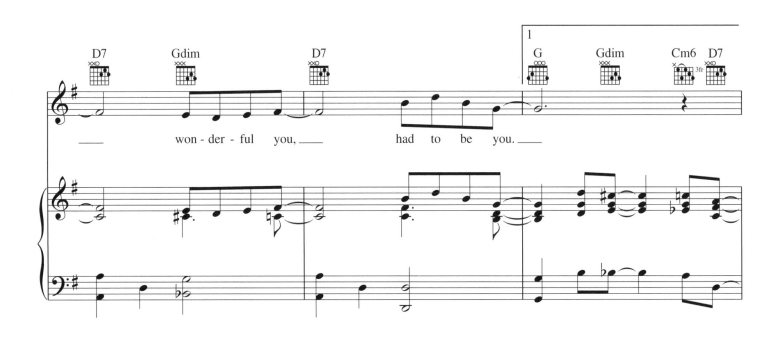

won-der-ful you, ___ had to be you. ___

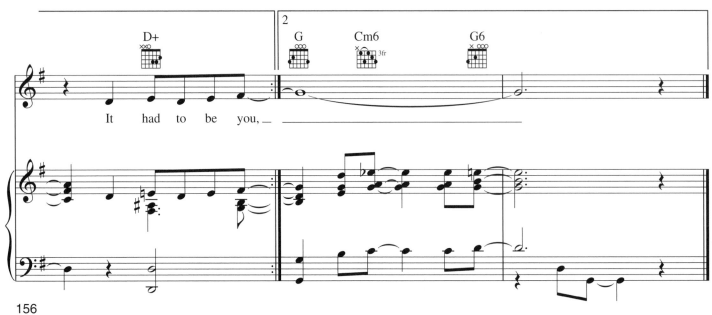

It had to be you, ___ _____

156

Just Friends

Lyrics by Sam M. Lewis

Music by John Klenner

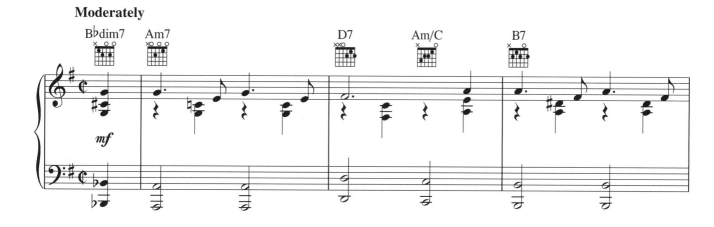

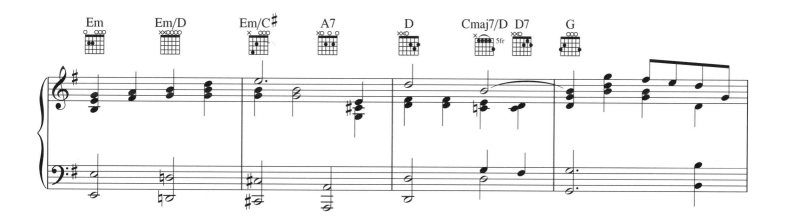

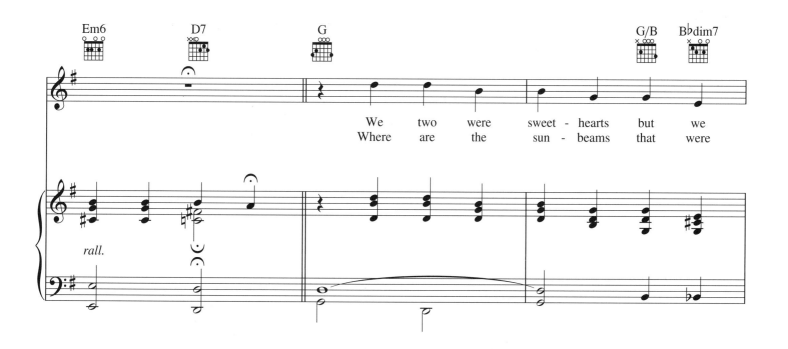

We two were sweet-hearts but we
Where are the sun-beams that were

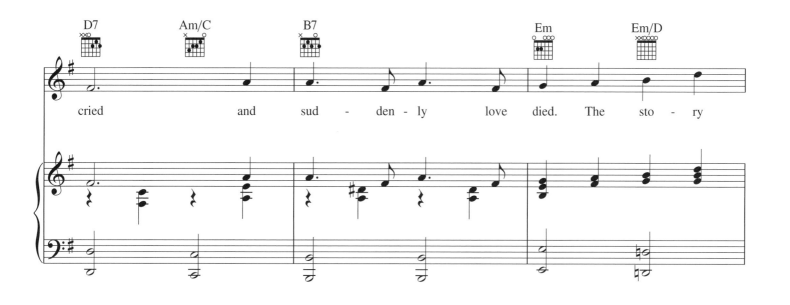

cried and sud - den - ly love died. The sto - ry

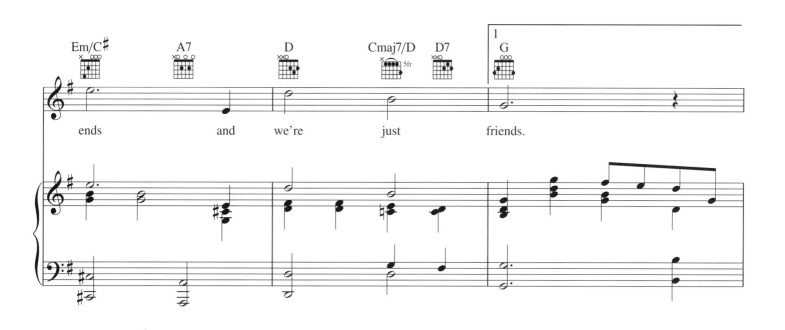

ends and we're just friends.

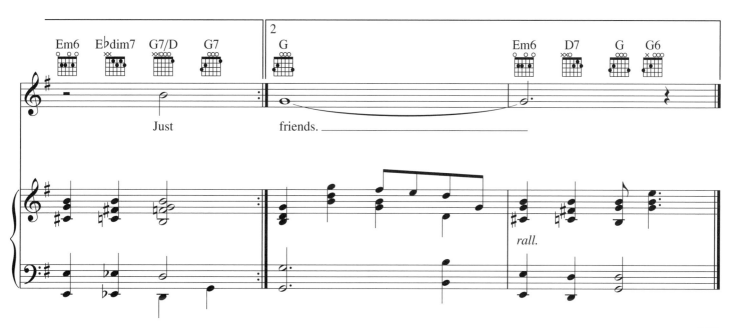

Just friends. Just friends.

rall.

Just One of Those Things

from HIGH SOCIETY

Words and Music by
Cole Porter

Let There Be Love

Lyric by Ian Grant

Music by Lionel Rand

Long Ago
(And Far Away)
from COVER GIRL

Words by Ira Gershwin

Music by Jerome Kern

up and down my spine, A - lad - din's lamp is mine, the dream I

dreamed was not de - nied me. Just one look and then I

knew _____ that all I longed for long a - go was

you.

you. _____

Love Walked In

Music and Lyrics by
George Gershwin and Ira Gershwin

magic mo - ment and my heart seemed to know

that love said "Hel - lo," though not a

word was spo - ken. One look and I for -

got the gloom of the past. One look and I had

found my fu - ture at last. One look and I had found a world com - plete - ly new when love walked in with you. you.

Lover, Come Back to Me

from THE NEW MOON

Lyrics by Oscar Hammerstein II

Music by Sigmund Romberg

Lullaby of Birdland

Words by George David Weiss

Music by George Shearing

Mack the Knife
from THE THREEPENNY OPERA

English Words by Marc Blitzstein
Original German Words by Bert Brecht

Music by Kurt Weill

sight. _____ When the shark bites _____ with his teeth, dear, _____ scar - let bil - lows _____ start to spread. _____ Fan - cy gloves, though, _____ wears Mac - heath, dear, _____ so there's not a _____ trace of red. _____ On the

C6　　　　　　　　　　　　　　Dm　　　　　　　　Dm7

tug - boat _____ by the riv - er _____ a ce-
Taw - dry, _____ Jen - ny Div - er, _____ Pol - ly

G9　　　　　　　　　　　　　C6

ment bag's _____ drop - ping down; _____ the ce-
Peach - um, _____ Lu - cy Brown; _____ oh, the

Am　　　　　　Am7　　Dm7

ment's just _____ for the weight, dear. _____ Bet you Mack - ie's _____
line just forms _____ on the right, dear, _____ now that Mack - ie's _____

G7　　1. C6　　　　　　　　　　G9　　2. C6

_____ back in town. _____ Lou - ie
_____ back in town. _____

rall.

The Man I Love

from LADY BE GOOD

Music and Lyrics by
George Gershwin and Ira Gershwin

make him stay.
He'll look at me and smile,
I'll un-der-stand;
And in a lit-tle while
He'll take my hand;
And though it seems ab-surd,
I know we both won't say a word.
May-be I shall meet him Sun-day, May-be Mon-day may-be

Mood Indigo

from SOPHISTICATED LADIES

Words and Music by
Duke Ellington, Irving Mills
and Albany Bigard

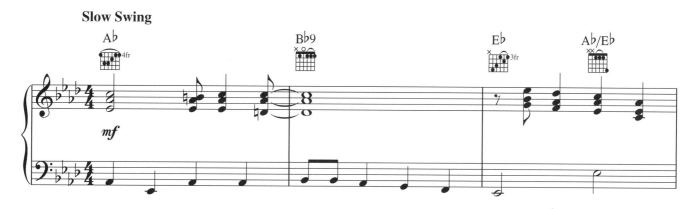

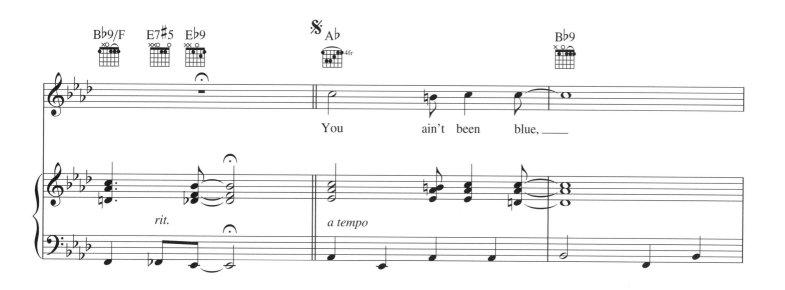

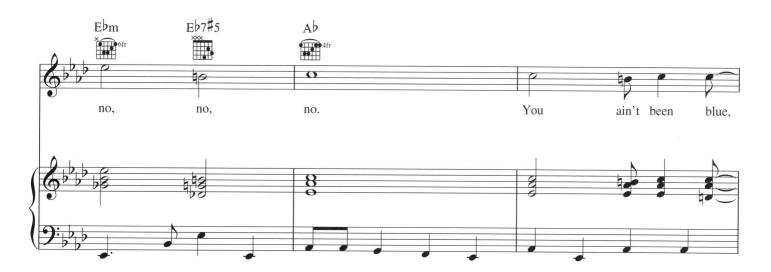

I'm just a soul who's blu- er than blue___ can be.

When I get that mood in- di- go, ___

I could lay me down and die.

die.

"Go 'long blues."

Moonlight in Vermont

Words by John Blackburn

Music by Karl Suessdorf

ski trails on a moun tain - side, snow - light in Ver -

mont. Tel - e - graph ca - bles, they

sing down the high - way and trav - el each bend ___ in the

road. Peo - ple who meet ___ in this

198

My One and Only Love

Words by Robert Mellin

Music by Guy Wood

My Romance
from JUMBO

Words by Lorenz Hart

Music by Richard Rodgers

Refrain *(smoothly, with expression)*

We don't need that flow - 'ry fuss, no sir, Ma - dam, not for us. My ro - mance does - n't have to have a moon in the sky, my ro - mance does - n't need a blue la - goon stand - ing by; no

On Green Dolphin Street

Lyrics by Ned Washington

Music by Bronislau Kaper

209

heart. _____ When I re-

call the love I found on, I could kiss the

ground on _____ Green Dol - phin Street. _____

Street. _____

One for My Baby

(And One More for the Road)

from the Motion Picture THE SKY'S THE LIMIT

Lyric by Johnny Mercer

Music by Harold Arlen

'Round Midnight

Words by Bernie Hanighen

Music by
Thelonious Monk and Cootie Williams

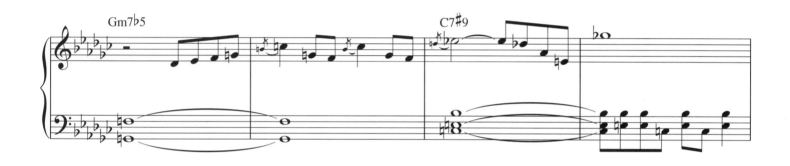

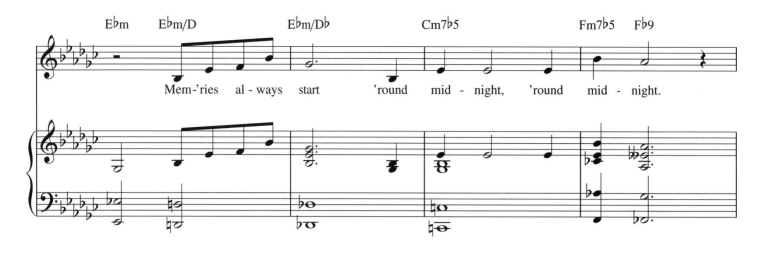

Mem-'ries al - ways start 'round mid - night, 'round mid - night.

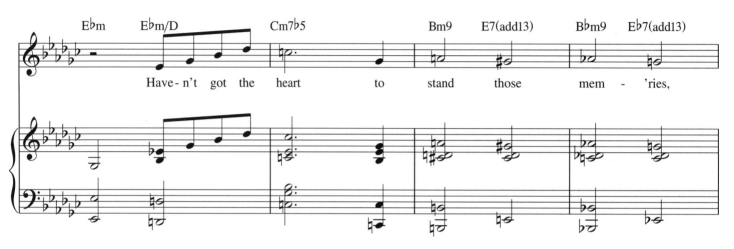

Have - n't got the heart to stand those mem - 'ries,

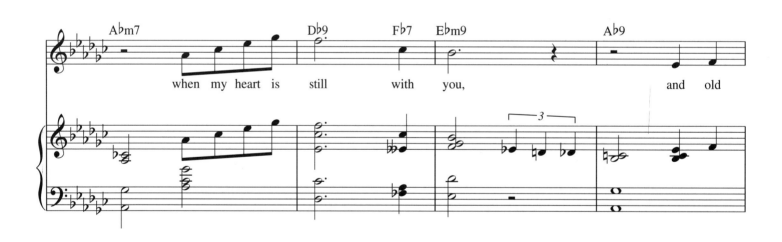

when my heart is still with you, and old

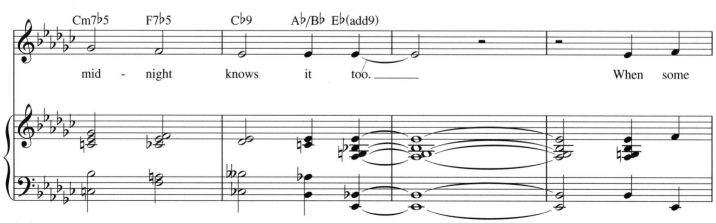

mid - night knows it too. _____ When some

218

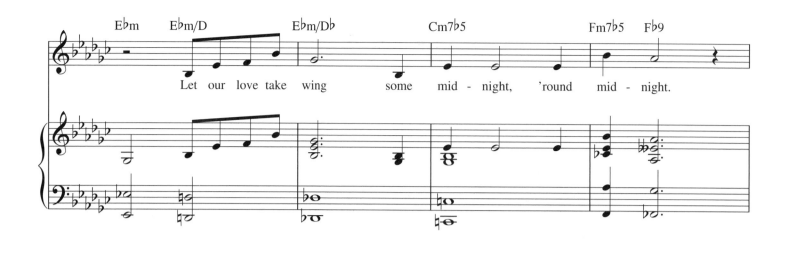

Let our love take wing some mid - night, 'round mid - night.

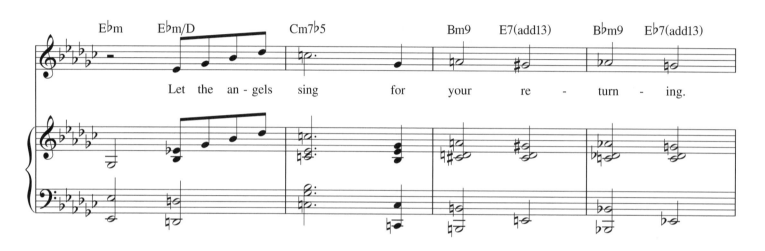

Let the an - gels sing for your re - turn - ing.

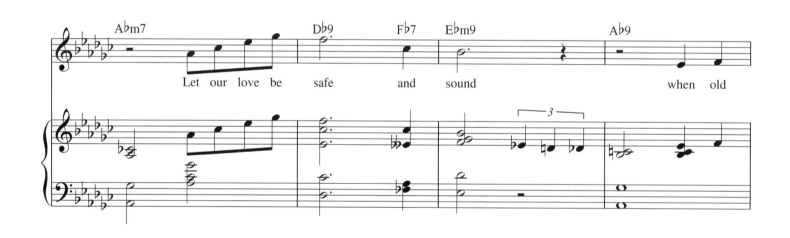

Let our love be safe and sound when old

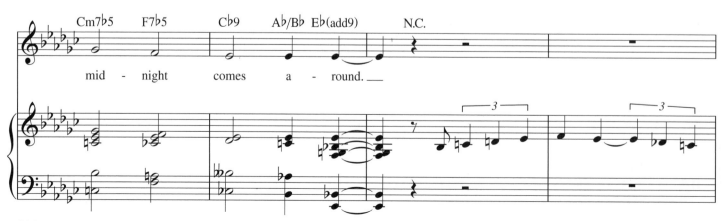

mid - night comes a - round. ___

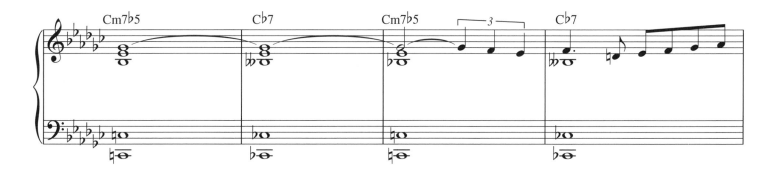

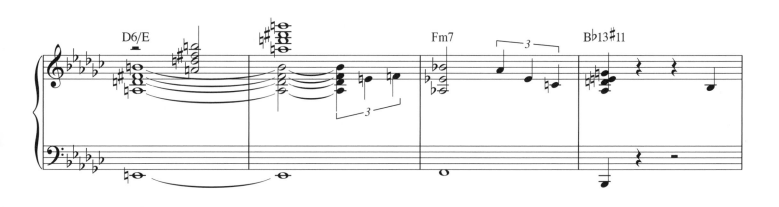

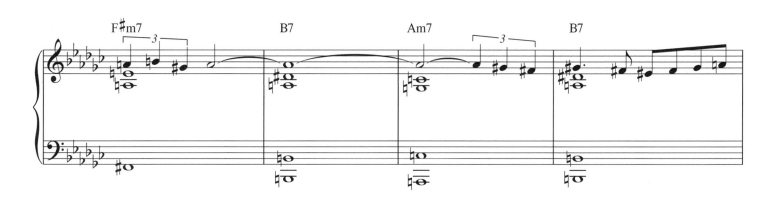

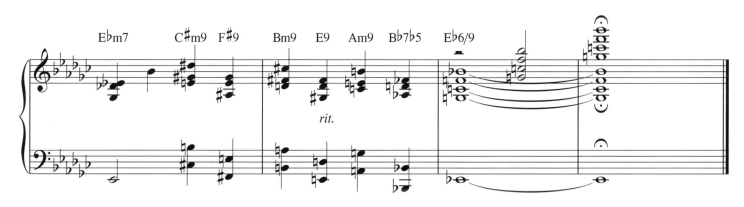

Satin Doll
from SOPHISTICATED LADIES

Words by
Johnny Mercer and Billy Strayhorn

Music by Duke Ellington

Sentimental Journey

Words and Music by
Bud Green, Les Brown
and Ben Homer

Slowly

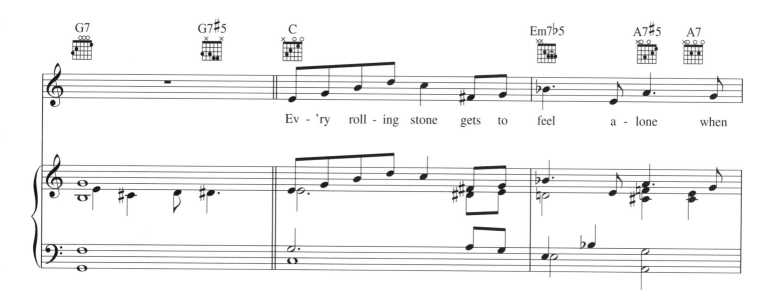

Ev - 'ry roll - ing stone gets to feel a - lone when

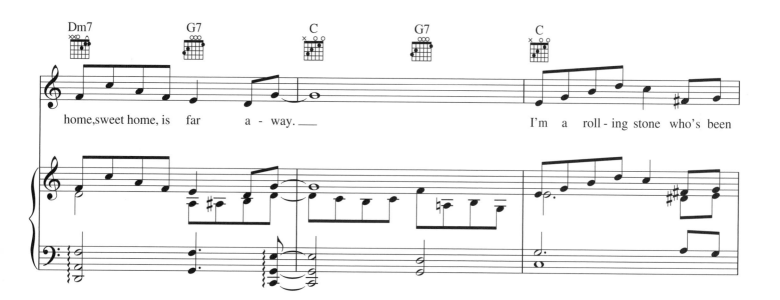

home, sweet home, is far a - way. ___ I'm a roll - ing stone who's been

so a - lone   un - til   to - day.

Gon - na take a sen - ti - men - tal jour - ney,   gon - na set my

heart at ease. __   Gon - na make a sen - ti - men - tal jour - ney

to re - new old mem - o - ries. __   Got my bag,   I

got my res - er - va - tion, spent each dime I could af - ford.

Like a child in wild an - tic - i - pa - tion, long to hear that

"All __ a - board." __ Sev - en, _____ that's the time we leave, at

sev - en _____ I'll be wait - in' up for heav - en, _____

227

count - in' ev - 'ry mile of rail - road track __ that takes me back. __

Nev - er thought my heart could be so "yearn - y." Why did I de -

cide to roam? __ Got - ta take a sen - ti - men - tal jour - ney,

sen - ti - men - tal jour - ney home. __ jour - ney home. __

The Shadow of Your Smile

Love Theme from THE SANDPIPER

Words by Paul Francis Webster

Music by Johnny Mandel

many a day and many a lone-ly mile. The ech-o of a
pi-per's song the shad-ow of a smile.

Moderately, slow 4

The shad-ow of your smile when you are
gone Will col-or all my dreams and

Someone to Watch Over Me

from OH, KAY!

Music and Lyrics by
George Gershwin and Ira Gershwin

lost in the wood. I know I could Al - ways be good

To one who'll watch o - ver me. _____

_____ Al - though he may not be the man some Girls

think of as hand - some To my heart he

Speak Low

from the Musical Production ONE TOUCH OF VENUS

Words by Ogden Nash

Music by Kurt Weill

Spring Is Here

from I MARRIED AN ANGEL

Words by Lorenz Hart

Music by Richard Rodgers

Stars Fell on Alabama

Words by Mitchell Parish

Music by Frank Perkins

Moon - light and mag - no - lia,   star - light in your hair,

all the world a dream come true. Did it real - ly hap - pen,

was I real - ly there, was I real - ly there with you?

We lived our lit - tle dra - ma, we kissed in a field of

white, and stars fell on Al - a - bam - a last

Stella by Starlight

from the Paramount Picture THE UNINVITED

Words by Ned Washington

Music by Victor Young

Moderately slow

Have you seen Stel - la by star - light, stand - ing a - lone,

moon in her hair? Have you seen Stel - la by star - light,

when have you known rap - ture so rare? The song

Steppin' Out with My Baby

from the Motion Picture Irving Berlin's EASTER PARADE

Words and Music by
Irving Berlin

Street of Dreams

By Sam M. Lewis
and Victor Young

Mid - night, _____ you heav - y lad - en, it's
Mid - night, _____ look at the stee - ple, it's

mid - night. _____ Come on and trade in your old dreams for new, your
mid - night. _____ Un - hap - py peo - ple, it's ring - ing with joy, it's

smil-ing on the street of dreams.
smil-ing on the street of dreams.

Love laughs at a king, kings don't mean a

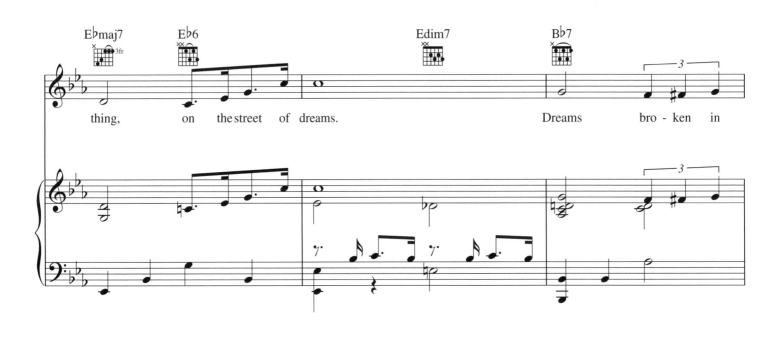

thing, on the street of dreams.

Dreams bro-ken in

two can be made like new

on the street of dreams.

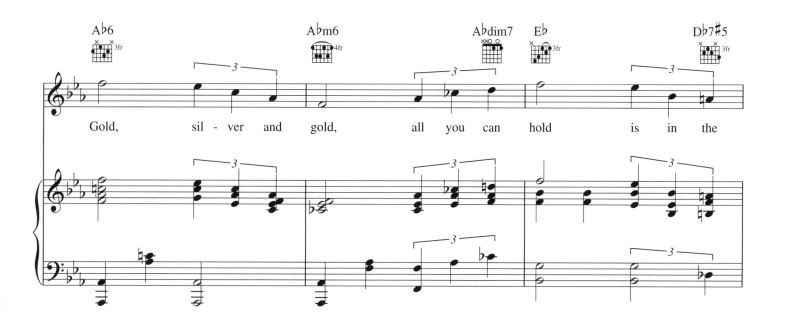

Gold, sil - ver and gold, all you can hold is in the

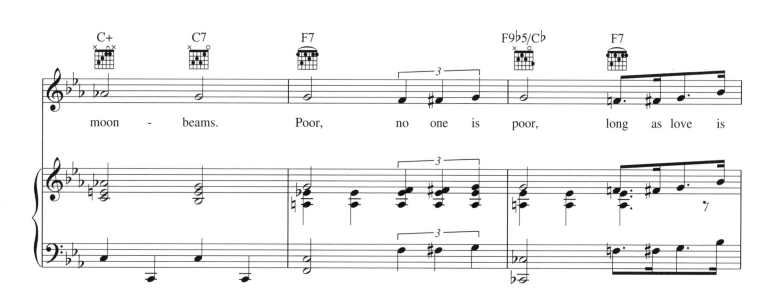

moon - beams. Poor, no one is poor, long as love is

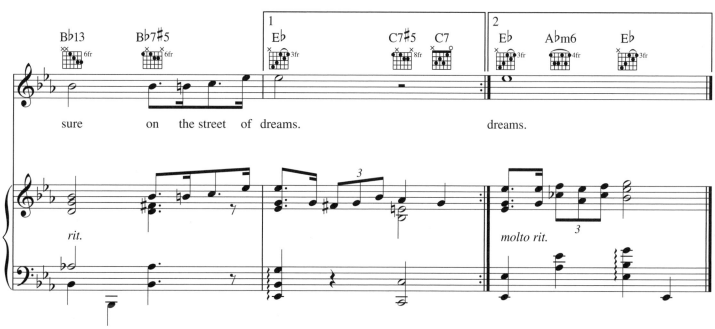

sure on the street of dreams. dreams.

Summertime

from PORGY AND BESS®

Music and Lyrics by
George Gershwin, Du Bose and Dorothy Heyward
and Ira Gershwin

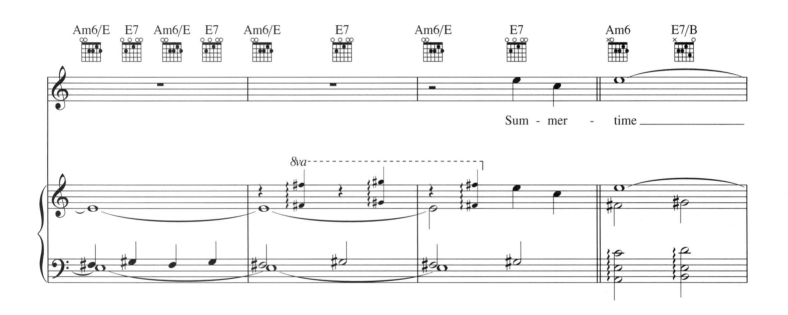

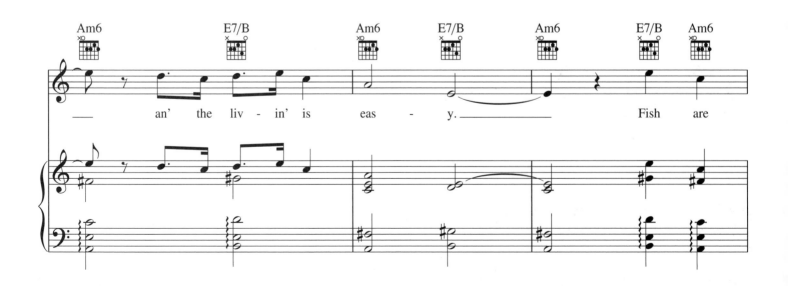

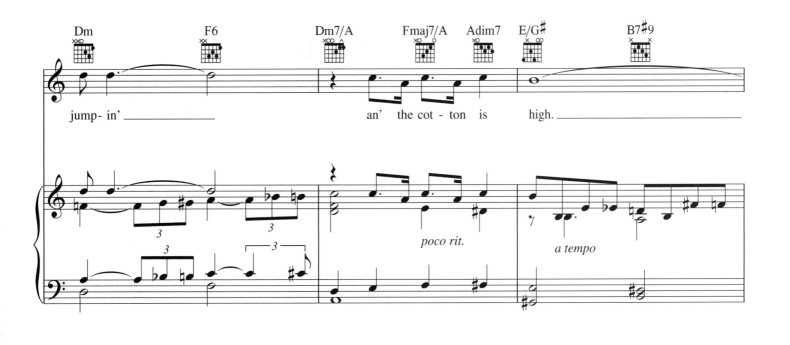

jump - in' ___ an' the cot - ton is high. ___

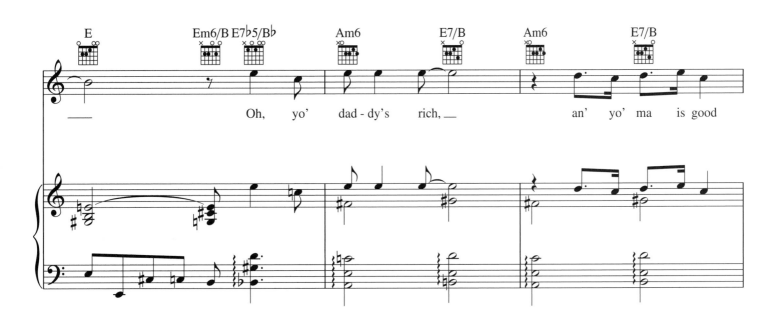

Oh, yo' dad - dy's rich, ___ an' yo' ma is good

look - in'. ___ So hush, lit - tle ba - by, don' __ yo'

That Old Black Magic

from the Paramount Picture STAR SPANGLED RHYTHM

Words by Johnny Mercer

Music by Harold Arlen

kiss _____ can put out the fire. _____ For
you're the __ lov - er I have wait - ed __ for, _____ the
mate that __ fate _____ had me cre - at - ed __ for, _____ and
ev - 'ry __ time _____ your lips meet mine, _____ dar - ling,

There Is No Greater Love

Words by Marty Symes

Music by Isham Jones

271

There is no great - er thrill than what you bring to me, _____ no sweet - er song than what you sing to me. _____ You're the sweet - est thing I have ev - er known,

They Say It's Wonderful

from the Stage Production ANNIE GET YOUR GUN

Words and Music by
Irving Berlin

set my heart a-glow.
heard is real-ly so.

Wish I knew if the things I hear are so.
I've been there once or twice and I should know.

Slowly

They say that fall-ing in love is
You'll find that fall-ing in love is

rall.

a tempo

won-der-ful; _____ it's won-der-ful, _____ so they
won-der-ful; _____ it's won-der-ful, _____ *Annie:* so you

This Can't Be Love

from THE BOYS FROM SYRACUSE

Words by Lorenz Hart

Music by Richard Rodgers

The Very Thought of You

Words and Music by
Ray Noble

I don't need your por-trait, dear, _____
I'm su-ing your for dam-ag-es, _____

_____ to call _____ you to mind, _____ For sleep-ing or
_____ ex-cus-es won't do, _____ I'll on-ly be

wak-ing, dear, _____ I find; _____
sat-is-fied _____ with you; _____

With a slow, easy swing (♩♪ = ♩♪)

The ver-y thought of you, _____ and I for-

get to do _____ the lit - tle

or - di - nar - y things that ev - 'ry - one ought to do. _____

_____ I'm liv - ing in a kind of day - dream, I'm

hap - py as a king, and fool - ish tho' it

Watch What Happens

from THE UMBRELLAS OF CHERBOURG

Original French Text by Jacques Demy
English Lyrics by Norman Gimbel

Music by Michel Legrand

Give that deep love to you _____ and what mag-ic you'll

see: Let some-one give his heart, Some-

one who cares like me. _____

me. _____

Yesterdays

from ROBERTA
from LOVELY TO LOOK AT

Words by Otto Harbach

Music by Jerome Kern

The Way You Look Tonight

from SWING TIME

Words by Dorothy Fields

Music by Jerome Kern

You'd Be So Nice to Come Home To

from SOMETHING TO SHOUT ABOUT

Words and Music by
Cole Porter

You've Changed

Words and Music by
Bill Carey and Carl Fischer

299

Slowly, with feeling

hon-est-ly be-lieve that you are bored. You've changed, that

spar-kle in your eyes is gone, your smile is just a care-less

yawn, you're break-ing my heart, you've changed.

You've changed, your kiss-es now are so bla -